# Thank you

for choosing
this Rivista Lyn Journal

If you enjoyed this journal
please consider leaving
us a review

www.ingramcontent.com/pod-product-compliance
Lightning Source LLC
Chambersburg PA
CBHW070431290526
45791CB00005B/1927
* 9 7 8 1 0 7 2 3 3 2 5 0 3 *